THE BUTCHER OF BARABOO

Marisa Wegrzyn

BROADWAY PLAY PUBLISHING INC
224 E 62nd St, NY NY 10065-8201
212 772-8334 fax: 212 772-8358
BroadwayPlayPub.com

THE BUTCHER OF BARABOO
© Copyright 2015 by Marisa Wegrzyn

cover art by Eric Triantafillou

I S B N: 978-0-88145-621-9

First printing: January 2016

Book design: Marie Donovan
Page make-up: Adobe Indesign
Typeface: Palatino
Printed and bound in the U S A

THE BUTCHER OF BARABOO was commissioned by
Steppenwolf Theatre Company.

THE BUTCHER OF BARABOO was developed and
produced in Steppenwolf Theatre Company's First
Look Repertory of New Work (Artistic Director,
Martha Lavey; Executive Director, David Hawkanson,
Director of New Play Development, Edward Sobel)
in Chicago, Illinois, in Summer 2006. The cast and
creative contributors were as follows:

VALERIE .... Annabel Armour
MIDGE ....Rebecca Sohn
GAIL ....Natalie West
DONAL ....John Judd
SEVENLY ....Danica Ivancevic

Director ....Dexter Bullard
Set design ....Jack Magaw
Lighting design .... J R Lederle
Costume design ....Tatjana Radisic
Sound design..Martha Wegener
Dramaturg ....Sarah Gubbins
Stage manager ....Lauren V Hickman

THE BUTCHER OF BARABOO was premiered Off-Broadway by Second Stage Theatre Uptown (Artistic Director, Carole Rothman; Executive Director, Ellen Richard), in New York City in Summer 2007. The cast and creative contributors were as follows:

VALERIE ....Debra Jo Rupp
MIDGE ....Ashlie Atkinson
GAIL .... Welker White
DONAL ....Michael Countryman
SEVENLY .... Ali Marsh

Director ....Judith Ivey
Set design ....Beowulf Boritt
Lighting design .... Jeff Croiter
Costume design .... Andrea Lauer
Sound design .... Ryan Rumery
Stage manager .... Lori Ann Zepp

CHARACTERS & SETTING

VALERIE, *female, 50s. A butcher.*
MIDGE, *female, 32. A pharmacist.* VALERIE's *daughter.*
GAIL, *female, mid/late 40s. A cop.* VALERIE's *sister-in-law.*
DONAL, *male, 50s.*
SEVENLY, *female, 30s.*

A house in Baraboo, Wisconsin, U S A. February.

ACT ONE

Scene One

(The kitchen and living-room of VALERIE'S *small house in Baraboo, Wisconsin on a cold February morning. The room is comfortable, accented with kitchen kitsch: cow potholders, souvenir mugs, a wall calendar of puppy dogs, etc. There's an impressive array of cutlery. A meat cleaver juts from a butcher block.)*

*(*VALERIE *sits at the table with a mug of coffee. She reads the morning paper.)*

*(*MIDGE *enters, pajamas, bed-head. She sets out a bowl, a spoon, and a box of Count Chocula. She opens the fridge and takes out a gallon of milk. There is only a splash left. She holds it out for Valerie to see, shakes it.)*

VALERIE: You know where the grocery store is.

*(*MIDGE *puts the milk back in the fridge. She pulls out a 2 liter bottle of pop and sits at the table. She opens the cereal box and fishes the prize out; this will be the highlight of her day. She pours the cereal in the bowl and pours the pop on the cereal and eats.)*

VALERIE: Why's it you're coming in so late now, no explanation to me, why is that, Midge, hm? When I've gone and made dinner and you're not even here. I heard a rumor from Mary Berwyn and I'm not one to believe gossip straight out, especially from that

woman, so why don't you tell me direct. What were
you doing behind the Jr. High school last night?

*(MIDGE gets up and opens the can of Maxwell House coffee.
It's almost empty, so she gets a full bag of Starbucks coffee
and prepares to pour it in the Maxwell House can.)*

VALERIE: The heck you're doing? What are you doing
to my coffee?

MIDGE: Was empty.

VALERIE: In *my* Maxwell House?

MIDGE: Where I always put my coffee.

VALERIE: Always?

MIDGE: Yeah.

VALERIE: The heck can't you scoop it out of the bag,
why are you putting it my…that's not decaf. You know
I don't drink caffeine.

MIDGE: Yeah, I guess.

VALERIE: Yeah, you guess? Mess up my coffee again
and yeah you can guess how many chops it takes my
cleaver to chop your hand clean off.

MIDGE: Starbucks is a step-up. Seattle refined the coffee
drinking experience.

VALERIE: This is not Seattle. This is America.

MIDGE: Seattle is in America.

VALERIE: But are we in Seattle?

MIDGE: We're in Wisconsin.

VALERIE: We are in Wisconsin.

MIDGE: Which is also in America like Seattle which is
also in America.

VALERIE: You know I don't drink caffeine.

MIDGE: You do now.

(VALERIE *takes the coffee bag, picks up her meat cleaver, slams the Starbucks bag on the butcher block, and cleaves the Starbucks with her meat cleaver.*)

MIDGE: *(Smoldering)* That is Fair Trade Coffee.

VALERIE: What is Fair Trade Coffee?

MIDGE: Fair Trade Coffee is expensive is what Fair Trade Coffee is.

VALERIE: How much does it cost?

MIDGE: It is very expensive. That particular bag I got for free. But normally it's twelve dollars a pound, plus tax, so thirteen dollars about.

VALERIE: Well it's half off now.

(MIDGE *salvages her coffee then returns to her breakfast.*)

VALERIE: These folks moving in next door, you'll see out there the moving trucks, these are nice and respectable people and I'd like it for you to be nice and respectable in return. Do you know what a nice and respectable person *doesn't* do? A nice and respectable person doesn't sell stolen pharmaceuticals behind the Junior High school to twelve-year-old children.

MIDGE: They're not twelve-year-olds, Mom. They're fourteen.

VALERIE: They are children, and stealing is wrong.

MIDGE: You steal stuff from work all the time.

VALERIE: Meat is different, meat is food. I am speaking the differ between food and drugs. Food and drugs have nothing in common.

MIDGE: The Food and Drug Administration.

VALERIE: Do you know what sort of law you could be dealing with if you get caught?

MIDGE: Aunt Gail, oh yeah, she's a regular *C S I: Baraboo.*

VALERIE: Not nice to make fun. Your Aunt Gail has feelings.

MIDGE: I have feelings too when she throttles me with the newspaper, you know what that feels like? Maybe you don't think current events hurt, but when they're all rolled up? And for no reason at all she hits me.

VALERIE: Oh, no reason?

MIDGE: None that I'm aware of.

VALERIE: None that you're aware of. Not even the time you made a crack about her hair, then asked which cop she thought she was, Cagney or Lacey? Or the time you plastered her squad car in neon Post-It notes? And she certainly had no reason to give you a smack when you replaced the bullets in her gun with jelly beans. Now I won't say a word to Gail about the drugs and the Junior High kids. I won't turn this into a matter of police business if you say you'll stop selling drugs to children. And I want you to say it like you mean it.

MIDGE: I will stop selling drugs to children.

VALERIE: Did you mean it?

MIDGE: Yep.

VALERIE: You're a young woman, Midge. Get over this juvenile carry-on and find a nice man, have some nice kids of your own. You can find a good man. You're… attractive…in your own…unique way. For god sake, you are thirty-two.

MIDGE: You said I was a young woman.

VALERIE: Well you're thirty-two. Just about everyone you went to high school with is married. Even that boy who walked with you at graduation, that retarded boy. He's getting married. If a retarded boy can get married, it bodes well for you. You can do better than this.

MIDGE: What's "this"?

VALERIE: *(Gestures to whatever)* This. There's a whole world out there for you. You don't need to be living at home with me.

MIDGE: You don't appreciate my company.

VALERIE: Sweetheart. Sometimes I don't, you're right.

MIDGE: Thought you were lonely now that Dad is gone.

(GAIL appears at the kitchen door, knocks, lets herself in. She is in her cop uniform and winter cop gear.)

GAIL: You wouldn't have any a those good fillets left, Valerie, would you now?

VALERIE: Not on my person at the moment.

GAIL: Eddie really loves those fillets and when you get any extra T-bones, Eddie really loves those T-bones.

VALERIE: Yes, Eddie loves anything he doesn't have to pay for.

GAIL: That is so true. Cold out there, isn't it! And those poor movers next door, they must be freezing. Although they get warm, moving around like that, lifting heavy boxes and pull-out couches and tricycles you really should lock your door. I walked right in, anybody could walk right in, who-knows-who could waltz in here while you're asleep. Chop you in the neck with one of those dealies *(Meat cleaver)* happens all the time.

VALERIE: When exactly does it happen all the time?

GAIL: Ohhhh right let me pull out my dossier on neck chopping statistics in the greater Sauk County region. Happens all the time in general I'm saying. You and your cutlery. I only have me this here pocket knife, birthday present from Frank years back. Suits me just fine.

VALERIE: What, that little piss-ant thing?

GAIL: You wouldn't be thinking it so piss-ant sticking out of your neck. Oooh Starbucks! I don't drink the stuff myself, the Starbucks, but I could sit inside one of those shops for hours, listening to Norah Jones.

(VALERIE *has gotten a milk gallon filled with blood from the fridge and sets it in front of* GAIL.)

GAIL: —what in the holy heck is that.

VALERIE: Gallon of blood. ...The one you asked for?

GAIL: Ohh right right right, but Valerie, I won't be needing it til the Spring.

VALERIE: Made it sound you needed it now, I got it now.

GAIL: I can see you got it now but I don't need it til Spring. Y'know, I don't think you ever raised an eyebrow at my request. Don't you think it strange I request a gallon of blood?

VALERIE: I assumed it was for Eddie. The backwards lout will drink anything, won't he?

MIDGE: Oh snap.

VALERIE: Midge, what did I tell you about making fun.

MIDGE: ...you made fun, I went "oh snap".

VALERIE: Well it's not nice of you to laugh at Gail's stupid husband.

GAIL: Eddie is not stupid. A little not very smart sometimes, but that's far different from stupid.

VALERIE: Do you want the blood or not?

GAIL: Don't need it til Spring, for prom. See, in order to deter teenagers from the drinking and the driving around prom time, we like to stage the aftermath of a drunk-driving accident on the, uh, (*Points*) service road runs long the high school there, you know where I'm talking?

VALERIE: No.

GAIL: That road—you know where I'm talking right, that busted-up no-traffic road there, you know where I'm talking right?

MIDGE: I dunno, Aunt Gail, maybe I'll get it you keep pointing at the wall.

(GAIL *thwacks* MIDGE *hard with a bit of rolled-up newspaper*)

GAIL: So we get some crushed-up cars from the junkyard and kids from the drama club roll-playing the mangled victims— Always a real hit of the school year—but our morality tale seemed missing an element of nuance. So this year we're gonna spatter the drama kids in blood.

VALERIE: Seems a bit gratuitous.

GAIL: Oh you bet! Kids these days, you gotta shock it into them: don't drink and drive, don't do drugs, don't have sex, or you'll be dead. But kids are still drinking and crashing cars and I'm not convinced this program has any affect, really. Between you and me, I'm not sure it matters. *(Suddenly sullen)* …Not sure anything matters anymore…

(VALERIE *puts the gallon of blood back in the fridge.*)

GAIL: Whoa there girly, where you off to?

MIDGE: Getting ready for work.

GAIL: I'll be having a word with you before you're off to the pharmacy. 'K, dollface?

(MIDGE *exits.*)

VALERIE: What sort of word you need to be having with her?

GAIL: A matter that may concern her.

VALERIE: Police business?

GAIL: Mm. Police business.

(VALERIE *will pick up her meat cleaver as she speaks, twirl it in her hands.* GAIL *will discreetly put her hand near the gun in her hip holster, just in case.*)

VALERIE: Gail, I know we've had our differences since the day I married Frank.

GAIL: Now I don't begrudge you anything marrying my brother.

VALERIE: I wasn't saying you begrudged me that necessarily.

GAIL: If that's something you thought, I want to clear the air and say I don't begrudge you.

VALERIE: And I don't begrudge you either.

GAIL: *(Offended)* For what?

VALERIE: For what what?

GAIL: For what could you begrudge me for?

VALERIE: For whatever you don't begrudge me for.

GAIL: You know what I begrudge you for.

VALERIE: You said you didn't begrudge me.

GAIL: And I don't. I'm saying if I begrudged you something you know what I'd begrudge you for, but I don't, so it's moot.

VALERIE: *(Under her breath)* You're moot.

GAIL: What?

VALERIE: What?

GAIL: What did you say?

VALERIE: Hearing things.

GAIL: You said something, and I am not hearing things. I don't appreciate an insult to my intelligence. And even further, to take this further as I'm about to do,

Valerie, I don't appreciate you waving cutlery in my face.

VALERIE: Was a good four feet from your face and not in your face.

GAIL: Was near enough for a gal who knows how to wield cutlery and butcher people the way you do.

VALERIE: What did you say?

GAIL: I said near enough for a gal who wields cutlery and butcher animals the way you do.

VALERIE: You didn't say animals.

GAIL: I said animals.

VALERIE: No, you said—

GAIL: Animals.

VALERIE: Animals isn't what I heard.

GAIL: Look who's hearing things now, eh.

(VALERIE *slams the cleaver back into the butcher block.*)

VALERIE: What I'm saying is you don't need to take out your grudges on my daughter. Whatever police business you're here to talk to Midge about, let's consider the matter settled. We don't need to bring police business into the mix, I've already talked with her about it.

GAIL: You did?

VALERIE: Yes.

GAIL: And what did she say?

VALERIE: She said she'll stop.
…Because I know it might be a matter of police business, but she'll stop.
…She won't do it anymore because she'll get herself in a mess of trouble canoodling with Junior High kids.
…We're not talking about the same thing are we?

GAIL: What are *you* talking about?

VALERIE: I thought you said you were talking to Midge on police business.

GAIL: But what are *you* talking about?

VALERIE: Nothing. Noth—I thought we were talking something else.

GAIL: You thought we were conversing on some other matter sure. Sure.

VALERIE: Care for breakfast?

GAIL: I wouldn't say no to a splash of orange juice, would I?

VALERIE: Would you?

GAIL: No I would not.

(VALERIE *pours some juice for* GAIL.)

VALERIE: What sort of splash would you say no to? Splash of acid in your face?

GAIL: Careful now.

VALERIE: Figure of speech.

GAIL: There's no figure of speech about a splash of acid in my face.

VALERIE: Who are you, Emily Dickinson?

GAIL: I have read the poetry of Emily Dickinson and not one poem did she write about splashing acid in faces.

VALERIE: She should've though. Might make her poetry less boring.

(GAIL *laughs and sticks her hand in the cereal box, searching.*)

GAIL: She does bore the snot out of me.

VALERIE: Midge got the prize already.

GAIL: *(Removes her hand from the cereal box)* Now if we're talking poetry you know who's a *real* poet: Billy Joel. The man is dumped by his first record label, drinks a bottle of furniture polish in a botched suicide, turns his suicide note into the lyrics of *Tomorrow Is Today*. And that, Valerie, is the essence of true poetry by a true poet. What was the prize, like stickers or something?

VALERIE: You'll forget what I said about Midge?

GAIL: Would've been well forgotten without that business about splashing acid in my face.

VALERIE: Gail... Please.

GAIL: I don't like the world *canoodling*. But I trust you'll put a stop to whatever Midge is or isn't doing.

VALERIE: Thank you.

GAIL: She wouldn't do anything stupid.

VALERIE: She is a smart girl.

GAIL: Not so smart enough to keep from setting her hair on fire making soup. Out of a can, condensed. How's a person do something like that? I don't know. She managed.

VALERIE: Was twenty years ago, leave her alone.

GAIL: To be completely honest, Valerie, I'm not entirely comfortable thinking it's people like her who dispense pharmaceuticals to the population. Makes you wonder about all the incompetence in those professions we put our good faith in. *(She drops her gun.)*

VALERIE: Mm.

GAIL: And Midge is a little not very nice at that too, the way she treats people. If you're not very attractive, the least you could be is nice. You're forgiven an ugly mug if you have a good soul. You turned that girl of yours into a real B dash Itch, pardon my French, and I'm not just saying that because I'm still sore about the jelly beans.

VALERIE: Midge could be nicer, I suppose. She switched my Maxwell House for Starbucks.

GAIL: Oh but that's a step up.

VALERIE: She knows full well I don't drink caffeine. Full well. Does it anyway, does whatever she wants. Some days I could kill her.

GAIL: You don't mean that, sure.

VALERIE: Some days. Some days.

GAIL: If you were me and I were you, I wouldn't be saying such things, Valerie. And I wouldn't be saying them in such a way that it sounds like I could well mean it.

VALERIE: *(Pause)* Have people been talking about me?

GAIL: Now, now.

VALERIE: I've been taking notice. My regular customers not being so regular.

GAIL: Now, now.

VALERIE: Now now what "now, now," has there been gossiping?

(GAIL *moseys over to the wall calendar.)*

GAIL: Puppy dogs are cuter than the old calendar you had up here what was that last year's calendar you had up here what was that.

VALERIE: John Deere Tractors.

GAIL: Puppy dogs are cuter than John Deere Tractors.

VALERIE: Was Frank's calendar.

GAIL: Frank did love his John Deere.

VALERIE: He did, sure.

GAIL: He did. He did, sure. ...There we are. The 17th of February. Spot on. Guess the day had to come around sooner or later, didn't it. Poor Frank. What're you going to do with yourself today?

VALERIE: What I do with myself every Wednesday. Go to work.

GAIL: Hm.

VALERIE: Is there something you want to say to me, Gail? You say it to my face.

(DONAL *appears at the door and knocks.* VALERIE *opens the door)*

DONAL: Hey there neighbor.

VALERIE: Was wondering when you'd finally knock on my door.

DONAL: Busy morning, I was looking for a quick escape from the moving chaos. Of course saw Gail's squad car out there, hi Gail.

GAIL: Hi.

DONAL: This really does have to be a quick hello and get back, but I wanted to thank you for your invitation, Valerie, that's nice of you. My wife is insisting on bringing something. Sevenly is terribly excited to meet you.

GAIL: What invitation?

VALERIE: I invited Donal and his wife over for dessert, coffee.

GAIL: Why?

VALERIE: Because I'm nice.

GAIL: So you're all having a little get-together kinda thing, huh, little dessert, little coffee thing? *(To* DONAL*)* So that's why you asked me if I knew any babysitters, huh, you needed a babysitter so you could come here for a little dessert.

DONAL: Well...

GAIL: Suppose I was going to be having a word with Midge about that this morning. But clearly I wasn't invited to this family gathering, so.

DONAL: I'm sure Valerie wouldn't mind, would you Valerie, if, em....

VALERIE: Babysitting? *That's* the word you needed to have with Midge? Exactly how is babysitting a matter of police business?

GAIL: Well I am in uniform. So it was police business.

VALERIE: Not at all was it police business is more like it.

GAIL: It, yes, it did lean a bit towards not at all, didn't it. But it would be a shame if I had to mention the word *canoodling* to the chief of police, he just *hates* the word canoodling and especially hates people who engage in acts of canoodling.

VALERIE: *(Pause)* Would you like to join us for dessert, Gail?

GAIL: Oh, I dunno...

VALERIE: Please, Gail, join us for dessert Friday night.

GAIL: Well if you insist.

(MIDGE *enters, ready for work.*)

DONAL: Hi, Midge.

VALERIE: You remember your Uncle Donal?

DONAL: Been a long time, huh Kiddo. You were yay tall last time I saw you.

VALERIE: Would it kill you to give your uncle a hug?

(MIDGE *complies.*)

GAIL: Midge, you wanna babysit for Donal?

VALERIE: It's a couple hours and it's only six kids.

MIDGE: No.

VALERIE: Well you don't have to drag us to your dark place, you could just say "no."

MIDGE: I did say no.

VALERIE: Well you could say it nicer, with some nice inflection.

MIDGE: *(With jazz hands:)* No.

VALERIE: Don't forget milk on your way home.

MIDGE: Yeah right.

VALERIE: Yeah right right, don't forget.

(MIDGE exits.)

DONAL: I'm sure we'll find somebody to watch the kids, it's no problem. I should get back to the house. If there's anything I can do for you…I realize today must be hard for you. How are you holding up?

VALERIE: I'm doing okay.

DONAL: If you need anything…

VALERIE: Thank you, Donal.

DONAL: Gail, can I speak to you later about the parking ticket you left on the movers' truck.

GAIL: Law's the law, Donal.

DONAL: But I'm your brother.

(Lights)

Scene Two

lat week. Evening. DONAL, GAIL, SEVENLY *and*
V ALERIE *are in the midst of dessert.)*

DONAL: ...and so this story begins oh, let's see. This is like something something years ago I'm at. This was high school, and I know that was when you first met Frank wasn't it, Valerie. I remember clear as a bell Frank at the kitchen table. Has his notebook doing homework, and he looks up at me says there's this *girl*, and the look in his eyes goes all soft—I remember this one moment so clear about my brother—this *girl*. He says just like that. This girl in my biology class and we're lab partners and she's excited to dissect the frog. And then he blurts: and I'm going to marry her.

VALERIE: He did not say that.

DONAL: As God is my witness.

GAIL: I highly doubt Frank blurted anything.

DONAL: So Frank, as you know, was a quiet boy. Shy. Christmas vacation rolls around, I ask him, so have you even asked her on a date yet? I haven't said one word to her, he tells me. You're her lab partner, how can you not say one word to her? I don't know, he says, she seems to be okay with it. Frank! You like her! Ask her *something*! So what did he ask you?

VALERIE: Asked me if I wanted to go ice fishing.

DONAL: Who asks a girl to go ice fishing on a first date? Who does that?

VALERIE: I said yes, didn't I?

DONAL: You did. Do you remember that day, Gail? That day ice fishing and Valerie came with us. I was just thinking. So we were technically all on your first date with Frank. That's funny.

GAIL: Dad didn't like to take me ice fishing.

DONAL: He did take you.

GAIL: Took me that once, wouldn't take me again.

DONAL: You complained.

GAIL: I did not so.

DONAL: "Oh my toes. I have frostbite. There's a bear."

GAIL: I never said there's a bear, was Frank saying there's a bear when it was just fat Mr. Harris sitting on a bucket looking fat and bear-like. Boy Glenn's dad was fat wasn't he? Freak Show is what we called him. Morbidly obese is the polite term now. He had a heart attack on the toilet last year had to knock down a wall to get him out. That was Frank saying "there's a bear." I never said there's a bear.

DONAL: All right, Gail, you never said there was a bear, I was mistaken.

GAIL: I think you were mistaken, Donal.

DONAL: I don't suppose Frank kept up with the ice fishing, did he.

VALERIE: Was the odd time he'd pick up and go. Fish the day and that was enough for the year.

DONAL: Did he ever get you out on that cold lake with him again?

VALERIE: No. No.

(Silence)

SEVENLY: I love to hear stories of how people met. Me and Donal met through my brother, when they were on their Missions in Brazil.

DONAL: Honey, they know how we met.

SEVENLY: Valerie doesn't. Valerie and Frank didn't come out to the wedding.

DONAL: I'm sure she knows, we don't need to bore them.

SEVENLY: Are we boring you?

VALERIE: No, no.

GAIL: I'm a little bored.

SEVENLY: Oh no. You are?

GAIL: Little bit.

SEVENLY: Gail, how was it you and Eddie met?

VALERIE: Yes, tell her how you met Eddie.

SEVENLY: Do tell!

GAIL: They know how me and Eddie met.

SEVENLY: Oh, I don't.

VALERIE: Sevenly doesn't know.

DONAL: You have to tell it now.

GAIL: I was a rookie cop, I get a call to go on over to Mrs McGinty's house on Surrey Lane. Says she's hearing a thump coming from the roof, like a *(Thumps fist on table)* Every half hour or so a *(Thumps fist on table)* Thinks there's a burglar and would I check it out? So I go around the house, inside and out. I hear it… *(Thumps table)*… Then way across the way on 18ᵗʰ Street, there's a whoopin' and a hootin', some fellas got something going on. Eddie and Tommy Laroux and Jessie Berwyn and… they got this contraption set up in the backyard. *(Looks to VALERIE)* …you're just busting to tell what it was.

VALERIE: This thing looks like something Wile E Coyote would order out of the ACME catalogue.

DONAL: The infamous squirrel catapult.

VALERIE: Eddie likes to break it out on the 4ᵗʰ of July.

GAIL: I pull up and Eddie's smearing peanut butter in the bowl because you gotta lure the squirrels before you launch 'em onto rooftops. And I say, y'know, we got a complaint and you can't be launching squirrels onto Mrs McGinty's roof. So that's how I met Eddie. And then we got married.

SEVENLY: Were the squirrels okay?

GAIL: Squirrels bounce.

DONAL: I'm sure they were fine.

GAIL: Midge said she'd make an appearance tonight? Right Val?

VALERIE: Don't call me Val. I don't call you Gay.

GAIL: Don't call me Gay.

VALERIE: Then don't call me Val.

GAIL: How about I call you Ms Grumpy Pants, would you like that instead? Huh, Ms Grumpy Pants, who irons her trousers with grumpy starch and a hot grumpy iron.

SEVENLY: (Looking at VALERIE's meat cleaver) That's a big one! Sharp too, I bet, huh. Sharp. Donal, do you remember those knives I bought from the shopping channel and how dull and flimsy they turned out to be.

DONAL: Mm.

SEVENLY: They were so dull and flimsy I couldn't believe how dull and flimsy they were, they weren't sharp and sturdy like this. Those Q V C knives were just, oh, disappointing's the word.

VALERIE: Would you like to pick it up?

SEVENLY: Oh no, but thank you for the offer.

GAIL: What a weird thing to offer.

VALERIE: She was admiring it.

GAIL: Kids admire my gun, I don't let them take potshots at stop signs.

SEVENLY: I used to use a meat cleaver all the time. Everybody is so nice here! Donal had me worried, saying, now, Baraboo is not at all like Provo. And it's true, it's not at all like Provo, but everybody has been very welcoming.

DONAL: I'm sorry, honey, did you say you used to use one of those all the time?

SEVENLY: Oh yes! Don't you remember? I told you.

DONAL: No…

SEVENLY: I told you about the chickens. I didn't tell you about the chickens?

DONAL: Well I know your family raised chickens.

SEVENLY: *(To* GAIL *and* VALERIE*)* We raised chickens! I had a chicken and I named her Lulu. Lulu the Chicken. Oh she was a sweetheart. I'd read books to her.

GAIL: You read books to chickens?

SEVENLY: Well sure. To soothe them. They're not too critical if you read slow or mispronounce words or skip the boring parts to get to the good parts even if that means the book doesn't make sense. Chickens aren't so worried about narrative. *(Then self conscious)* Silly, I know. Reading to a chicken, who reads to a chicken.

VALERIE: That's not silly.

SEVENLY: I couldn't be the one to…my father took care of Lulu when it was her time to go.

(Quiet)

DONAL: Thank you for having us over. It's very kind of you.

SEVENLY: Yes, thank you for having us, Valerie. It's nice to feel welcome.

VALERIE: Ohh sure. Good brownies.

SEVENLY: These are Katherine Hepburn's brownies. Katherine Hepburn used this same recipe.

DONAL: I could eat a whole pan of these.

SEVENLY: Sometimes you have.

DONAL: Oh, now.

VALERIE: Tell me about your name, Sevenly. Does it mean what I think it means?

SEVENLY: I was the seventh child in my family.

GAIL: What's your younger sibling called? Eightly?

SEVENLY: There are no more after me. I'm the youngest in my family. *(Slight pause)* We all have big families. All my brothers and sisters I mean. And we always talked about having a big family.

DONAL: We're still deciding on the name for our next one. We've been thinking if it's a boy we'll name him Frank, you know. After, well, after Frank.

GAIL: You're expecting?

DONAL: No, no. No. Not yet. We're just planning ahead, right honey?

SEVENLY: Planning ahead.

DONAL: I suppose if it's a girl we could call her Frankie. What do you think of that?

SEVENLY: That's nice.

DONAL: We'll have at least one more when the time comes. I want to honor my brother's memory.

(GAIL rolls her eyes at this, scoffs.)

DONAL: Something you want to say, Gail?

VALERIE: I think it's a fine idea you're thinking to name the baby after Frank. Was a nice funeral you missed, Donal.

GAIL: This one didn't cry. I cried. This one didn't.

VALERIE: I don't need to make a public display.

GAIL: Well. At least you were there.

DONAL: I told you I couldn't leave Provo, and Sevenly couldn't travel being almost nine months along at the time, I explained all this to you.

GAIL: Donal, I'm not *accusing* you of anything. I'm not trying to make you feel *guilty*. When we find the body, then you can see Frank off proper. We can all see Frank off proper when we find the remains of him.

VALERIE: "When we find the body." Something I blame on shoddy police work.

GAIL: The heck you say shoddy police work, our police work is thorough and sound.

VALERIE: Thorough and sound like when the Petersen boy went missing.

GAIL: That wasn't a gaff in police procedure.

VALERIE: It took the circus cops a whole day to find him drunk asleep under a squad car in the police station parking lot.

GAIL: Well who sleeps under a squad car?! And we did find him. And it wasn't Jim running over his neck that killed him, but the transmission fluid dripped in his mouth he swallowed drunk asleep. All I'm saying is Devil's Lake is hardly a Great Lake. It's a great lake for fishing, sure, but where could a body go? We would've found it if that's where he was.

VALERIE: If you haven't found his body by now, you're not going to find it.

GAIL: *Oh?*

DONAL: Enough! …Enough… It's a terrible thing that happened. Frank is at rest—wherever he is. Let's leave it at that for tonight.

GAIL: I won't leave it at that, Donal, when I know full well she had some hand in our brother's death. How about that, Val?

VALERIE: You call me Val one more time I will cut your throat.

(Silence)

SEVENLY: Excuse me, where is your restroom?

VALERIE: Down the hall there, on the left. Hold the flush down, so.

*(*SEVENLY *exits.* GAIL *gets her coat.)*

VALERIE: I said I don't like you calling me Val. Donal, didn't I say I don't like her calling me Val. Gail, you push my buttons sometimes, you push and you push. I apologize for saying what I said about the throat cutting, I didn't mean it.

GAIL: *(To* DONAL*)* Don't ever say I didn't warn you.

VALERIE: Warned him, you warned him? There's no need for warnings here.

*(*MIDGE *enters. She has a plastic shopping bag filled with boxes of Sudafed.)*

MIDGE: Oh—hi.

GAIL: Whatya got there, Midge?

MIDGE: Nothing.

GAIL: Heard you've been getting in some trouble. Canoodling at the Junior High? *(She takes the bag from* MIDGE, *looks through the contents)* All this cold medication. Wow, Midge. You must have the world's worst cold.

MIDGE: Oh, it's terrible. *(Cough)*

GAIL: *(To* DONAL*)* Can you give us a minute here?

DONAL: Where do expect me to go?

GAIL: Go check on your wife make sure she's not reading to chickens.

*(*DONAL *exits.)*

GAIL: So who are these junior chemists you supply? Ohhh surprise surprise, you didn't think I knew a darn thing about your druggy buddies and the Meth labs? I want names, I don't care who you feel obligated to protect. Is it that Gordy Laroux who works at the Starbucks.

*(*MIDGE *doesn't respond.)*

GAIL: Yeah. That's what I thought.

*(*GAIL *leaves with* MIDGE's *bag, slamming the door)*

MIDGE: *(To* VALERIE*)* You said you weren't gonna tell her about the canoodling.

VALERIE: I didn't mean to use the word canoodling.

MIDGE: Aunt Gail is going to get me in trouble.

VALERIE: I didn't know you were mixed up dealing methamphetamines but I'm sure as heck glad I know now. Hooked on meth, the first thing to go is hygiene, I have seen the segments on *20/20.*

MIDGE: I thought me and you were going to look out for each other? I watch your back you watch mine. What happened to that?

*(*DONAL *and* SEVENLY *enter.* MIDGE *and* SEVENLY *have a moment of recognition—they've met, briefly, before)*

DONAL: Sevenly, this is my niece, Midge. Midge, my wife Sevenly.

SEVENLY: Hello.

VALERIE: Midge? Wasn't I saying something the other day about nice and respectable?

MIDGE: Golly, it sure is nice to meet you, Aunt Sevenly!

SEVENLY: Nice to meet you too.

DONAL: Midge is a pharmacist, at the what, the Walgreens?

MIDGE: Mm hm.

SEVENLY: Oh terrific, okay, sure.

MIDGE: You need anything from the pharmacy, you let me know. I get a good discount on Flintstones vitamins. For the kids.

DONAL: That's kind of you Midge.

MIDGE: Sure I'll be seeing you around the neighborhood. *(She exits.)*

SEVENLY: Donal, I think we should go home.

DONAL: You're right, it is getting to be about that time. Here. Why don't you go on ahead and pay the babysitter. *(Gives some money to SEVENLY)*

SEVENLY: You're not coming with?

DONAL: I'm going to help Valerie clean up. I'll be there in ten minutes.

SEVENLY: Okay. Don't forget the brownie pan. Thank you so very much, Valerie, this all was wonderful.

(SEVENLY exits. VALERIE cleans up. DONAL looks at the brownies)

DONAL: Gosh, I'm sick of these things. Sevenly makes them all the time. They're too rich for me.

VALERIE: You said you could eat a whole pan of them.

DONAL: She thinks I like them, so I say I like them. I don't want to hurt her feelings. The kids like 'em, though. Especially Lucas who's going through a phase about food that looks like poo.

VALERIE: How old?

DONAL: Five, he's five. That age, y'know.

VALERIE: Bet they keep you feeling young.

DONAL: Ahh well, some days.

VALERIE: Bet they're wonderful.

DONAL: Oh, they're terrors.

VALERIE: Terrors sure, that's why you're going for lucky number seven.

DONAL: God willing. They are wonderful kids. They really are.

VALERIE: Mm.

DONAL: Do you like Sevenly?

VALERIE: She's...very nice.

DONAL: Valerie...

VALERIE: You think I'm not being sincere I say that? She's a nice girl, she reads to chickens, you're a lucky man.

DONAL: You're never going to drop those chickens, are you?

VALERIE: Donal. I'm happy for you.

(DONAL *hugs* VALERIE, *a warm embrace. She melts into it.*)

DONAL: I don't believe one word of what Gail says. I *know* you had no hand in his death. Gail is upset, and when Gail gets upset she stays upset. She'll never forgive me for throwing her teddy bear into a lit barbeque and that was forty-some years ago. I was never very nice to her. She isn't the easiest person to love. Doesn't mean she's undeserving though. ... Valerie, you wouldn't happen to have any, em...

(VALERIE *gets a glass and a bottle of whiskey.*)

DONAL: What's Midge still doing here?

VALERIE: She lives here.

DONAL: Imagine she makes a good salary at the pharmacy.

VALERIE: You have some concern with my daughter?

DONAL: Just saying she could afford to be out of your hair. Or our out of your house at least, nevermind your hair. Which is very nice, by the way.

VALERIE: My house?

DONAL: Your hair. Looks nice.

(VALERIE *pours a drink for* DONAL.)

VALERIE: She's not going anywhere.

DONAL: She might, some day, want to.

VALERIE: …I don't think you need have concern with Midge, you mind your own kids.

DONAL: *(Re: drink)* Have one yourself.

VALERIE: Oh, offering me my own liquor now?

DONAL: Will you have a drink with me, Valerie?

VALERIE: I don't drink.

DONAL: Since when?

VALERIE: Last year.

DONAL: Well I don't drink anymore either. Don't tell. *(Drinks. Coughs)* Good lord.

VALERIE: It's a harsh brand. I keep it for the sentiment. Was Frank's favorite.

DONAL: You're not dwelling too much on it now?

VALERIE: No. No, not too much.

(Pause)

DONAL: Do you think he wanted to kill himself?

VALERIE: Would've been too big a commitment for Frank.

DONAL: What does that mean?

(VALERIE *waves it off.*)

DONAL: Now I want to know what you meant.

VALERIE: Well he could hardly commit to having a piece of toast. Like the easiest question in the world "do you want toast?" Either you want toast or you don't want toast. It's toast. But with Frank it was all hemming and hawing, "ohhhhh…I don't know. Maybe. Is it you're making some is why you asked? I just, ohh, I just don't know." And this was a lousy piece of toast and not a suicide, so you can stop thinking that way, suicide. He may have been a touch melancholy but that's all. That's all. Have another if you're going to have one. *(Drink)*

DONAL: Ohh, I don't know…

(VALERIE *pours* DONAL *another. He doesn't drink it.*)

DONAL: Can't shake the odd feeling that my brother is still out there. That feeling, y'know. Creeps up in the night.

VALERIE: You didn't come to the funeral and that's what funerals are for. Goodbyes and all.

DONAL: I'm sorry for whatever troubles you and Frank had in the end.

VALERIE: What makes you think we had troubles?

DONAL: Mister and Mrs Garrison, your old neighbors? Mentioned there was a, um. Disturbance. Before Frank disappeared.

VALERIE: Did the Garrisons also disclose you'll be dealing with seasonal water damage with that house?

A truck from Miller's Roofing was parked out front ever spring thaw, like clockwork. Bet they didn't tell you that, but I'm sure glad they took time to warn of one, single "disturbance". *(Pause)* I may have lost my temper.

DONAL: A shouting argument on the front lawn isn't that bad. In the grand scheme.

VALERIE: You always look on the bright side. *(Pause)* Frank lost his job, didn't tell me. One of my regular customers, Mindy, the librarian on the U W campus, said Frank had been spending his afternoons at the library. Couldn't be my Frank, I thought.

DONAL: Well, if he lost his job, I'm sure he was embarrassed is why he didn't tell you of his afternoons.

VALERIE: Frank was in the company of a young physics major, in a discreet corner of the library. I found this in the trunk of his car. A gift from his young friend.

(VALERIE gets a book. Steven Hawking's A Brief History of Time.)

DONAL: You know he's too polite to turn down a gift from a young woman.

(VALERIE opens the book, reads the inscription.)

VALERIE: "Why is it the way it is? If only we could explain. All my love in all the universe. ...Benjamin"

(Pause)

DONAL: Well. Are you sure this is, em. It could be just, em.

VALERIE: Donal. I am not a fool. *(She closes the book.)* It doesn't matter. Frank is gone.
Your wife is probably wondering where you are.

(DONAL puts on his coat.)

DONAL: Sevenly doesn't know anybody in town, and it would mean a lot to her to have a friend next door. She's a gentle soul. Would you be a friend to her? ...I'm sorry, you don't have to...

VALERIE: I can be a good friend.

DONAL: If she mentions anything you think I should know...

VALERIE: Like what?

DONAL: I don't know.

VALERIE: Worried about her?

DONAL: We've always been so open with each other, now it's all, em. The move has been stressful, you know?

VALERIE: Sure.

(Pause)

DONAL: If I had been the one to ask you to marry me, would you have said yes?

VALERIE: You didn't ask me to marry you. Was Frank who asked.

DONAL: But would you have said yes if I had asked?

VALERIE: You never asked. *(Pause)* Would you ever consider re-marrying?

DONAL: Is that something you're thinking about now? Re-marrying?

VALERIE: I'm saying if something were to happen to Sevenly. Would *you* re-marry?

DONAL: I don't want to think about that.

VALERIE: *(Regarding the whiskey)* Not going to finish?

DONAL: No.

VALERIE: Tell Sevenly I enjoyed meeting her, would you?

(DONAL *exits.* VALERIE *sets the book aside. She downs the whisky in* DONAL's *glass. She picks up her meat cleaver, sharpens it, and then thunks it back into the block.)*

Scene Three

(Later that evening. The lights in the kitchen are out. SEVENLY *opens the door and peeks her head into the kitchen.)*

SEVENLY: Hello? *(She enters. She picks up her brownie pan from the table. She senses someone in the room.)* Hello.

*(*MIDGE *turns on a light.)*

SEVENLY: The door was unlocked. Donal forgot to bring home the brownie pan.

MIDGE: We would've returned it.

SEVENLY: I just thought...I would get it tonight.

MIDGE: Good brownies.

SEVENLY: Oh. I'm. Glad you liked them.

MIDGE: They're very rich. Chocolatey. Like fudge almost.

SEVENLY: They're Katherine Hepburn's brownies. ...I didn't want to wake anybody.

MIDGE: You didn't.

SEVENLY: And the door was unlocked, so...

MIDGE: We don't lock our doors.

SEVENLY: You should lock your doors. We always lock our doors. Err on the side of caution. Have faith that god will keep you safe, but a sturdy deadbolt never hurts.

MIDGE: We have that stitched on a pillow.

SEVENLY: I. It's getting late and Donal doesn't know I left the house.

MIDGE: You need his permission to leave the house?

SEVENLY: No, but.

MIDGE: But.

SEVENLY: If he wakes up and I'm nowhere to be found I don't want him to worry that something happened to me.

MIDGE: He'd worry something had happened to you?

SEVENLY: Yes.

MIDGE: Something *bad* had happened to you.

SEVENLY: He's a worrier. He worries enough for the both of us. I worry too, but I'm not…"a worrier". In quotes. Not so much. How long have you been a pharmacist, Midge?

MIDGE: Two years.

SEVENLY: That's great, that's really great.

MIDGE: Junior pharmacist. I'm not one of the big dogs. I'm a peon. The big dogs peon me.

SEVENLY: I know what that's like. I used to work in an office. Accounting. I wasn't an accountant. I filed. I was good at filing. Very quick, accurate.

MIDGE: Are you cold?

SEVENLY: Ah. No. A little.

MIDGE: I bet your house is warmer than this.

SEVENLY: Yes.

MIDGE: That must be nice. *(Pause)* I had a dog liked to sleep on my feet kept my feet warm. Dog's been gone couple years now.

SEVENLY: What was your dog's name?

MIDGE: Steve.

SEVENLY: *(With a little laugh)* Steve? *(Pause)* Steve is a very nice dog name. *(Pause)* Pharmacists are sworn to customer privacy. Is that so? I read that somewhere. *Time* magazine, *Newsweek*.

MIDGE: It would be unprofessional to disclose information to outside parties.

SEVENLY: Oh. I was just curious when I inquired the other day at the pharmacy. I read about it and I was curious. That's all. I would appreciate it if you... if I could be sure you wouldn't...you wouldn't say anything to anybody. I would appreciate it very much.

MIDGE: It would be unprofessional of me to say anything.

SEVENLY: Thank you.

MIDGE: But... For future reference. If you want to be absolutely safe? Should make your inquiries at a pharmacy in another town. Here, people talk. They're terrible gossips. I hate everybody in this town. You'll probably like them, but I hate everybody.

SEVENLY: Hate is a strong word. It's a word I tell my children not to use.

MIDGE: Do you hate when your kids use it?

SEVENLY: Yes. No. Ooh, you got me.

MIDGE: I got you.

SEVENLY: Are you sure your mother's asleep, she can't hear us?

MIDGE: MOOOOOOOOOOOOOM!!!!

SEVENLY: Sssshhhh!!! Oh no, don't wake her.

MIDGE: Once she's down she's down for eight hours. Eight hours exactly. Ideally, adults should get eight hours. Ideally. What time do you need to get up tomorrow?

SEVENLY: Six.

MIDGE: (*Checks her watch*) Tomorrow is not going to be an ideal day for you.

SEVENLY: I am a very very nice person. That's what everybody at home says about me, that I'm very nice, that I'm a very nice good person who would never ever hurt anybody. And here I am. I feel terrible. I haven't been sleeping.

MIDGE: I can help you sleep.

SEVENLY: How can I sleep when I know I am going to hell.

MIDGE: You're not going to hell.

SEVENLY: I am, I am, it's people like me who go to hell.

MIDGE: You're not going to hell.

SEVENLY: I am, I am, I'm going to hell.

MIDGE: No you're not. Stop saying that. It's annoying.

SEVENLY: Have you ever killed anybody? Have you?

(*Pause*)

MIDGE: Here, have one of Katherine Hepburn's brownies.

(SEVENLY *knocks the brownies away.*)

SEVENLY: Fuck Katherine Hepburn's brownies! (*Shocked pause*) Oh my goodness. Oh my. I don't really feel that way about Katherine Hepburn's brownies. They're really very good brownies. I don't know what came over me. I'm not usually this way.

MIDGE: It's all right. Would you like some coffee? I have some made.

SEVENLY: I don't drink coffee.

MIDGE: Cream? Sugar?

SEVENLY: I don't…what do you usually put in it?

MIDGE: Two sugars, two and a half.

SEVENLY: That's fine.

MIDGE: How far along are you?

SEVENLY: I don't know.

MIDGE: You don't know for sure how far along you are?

SEVENLY: Not. Exactly. No.

MIDGE: Can you maybe take a guess? Makes a difference, I'm saying, what I can do for you.

SEVENLY: I don't know.

MIDGE: All right.

SEVENLY: Donal has been through this six times already. He'll know soon enough. I need to do something soon. I wouldn't be doing this if it weren't absolutely imperative.

(MIDGE *sets the mug in front of* SEVENLY.)

MIDGE: Here's what I can do. The pill you asked about the other day, it's emergency contraception. It's not abortive, it only prevents conception. The drug you need to terminate your pregnancy is RU-486, medical abortion. The manager of my pharmacy "forgets" to stock RU-486. So what I'm saying is I can't get it from my pharmacy. You need a doctor's prescription to… Hey. Hey. It's alright. Sevenly. Look at me. It's going to be all right. I know someone who will get it for you without going through a doctor. Nobody but me is going to have to know. Okay? Okay?

SEVENLY: Yeah, okay.

MIDGE: I'm not gonna tell, and don't you be having a break down either, feeling like you gotta tell *somebody*, especially don't let it slip around my mother because she's, like, *this close* to slapping a bumper sticker on her car, if you know what I mean.

SEVENLY: Who is this person, this someone you know.

MIDGE: Another pharmacist. Don't worry, I'll get it for you. It'll be a little more expensive then it would be otherwise, just so you know.

SEVENLY: Midge. Are you religious at all? Do you believe in God, in God's plan, in his will? Do you? I don't know you. I don't know anything about you. What kind of person are you?

MIDGE: I'm a very cool person.

SEVENLY: Does God think you're a very cool person?

MIDGE: The coolest.

SEVENLY: I've told you my biggest secret. Do you have anything you want to tell me?

MIDGE: Why. Like…why? Like, to reciprocate?

SEVENLY: Sure.

MIDGE: You might not like my biggest secret.

SEVENLY: Did you like my biggest secret? You didn't have to like it, it is what it is.

MIDGE: But I understand your secret. I understand fear. You're easy to comprehend.

SEVENLY: What is your biggest secret?

MIDGE: I like you.

SEVENLY: That's your biggest secret, that's, that's it? You like me, that's your biggest secret. Well that's not much of a secret.

MIDGE: You're okay with it that I like you?

SEVENLY: Well sure.

MIDGE: Would you want to do something sometime?

SEVENLY: What do you mean?

MIDGE: Would you like to go to lunch or see a movie sometime?

SEVENLY: Oh. Um. I don't know. I have six kids. If I want to do anything I need to get a sitter.

MIDGE: If I got you that sitter, if I paid for it, would you want to go to lunch and a movie some time?

SEVENLY: Um. Perhaps. Perhaps we can do that.

MIDGE: Perhaps perhaps or perhaps not a chance stop asking.

SEVENLY: Perhaps…

(Pause)

MIDGE: You don't want to finish the coffee? It's very good coffee. It's Fair Trade Coffee. It's expensive. But whatever. You want to leave so leave.

(MIDGE takes SEVENLY's coffee to the sink.)

SEVENLY: No, wait—I'll—it's cooled down some, I can drink it.

(MIDGE returns the coffee mug to SEVENLY. She drinks.)

MIDGE: It's very good coffee.

SEVENLY: It is, yes. Thank you. …What about…

MIDGE: What.

SEVENLY: Your pharmacist friend.

MIDGE: He's not my *friend.* He's someone I know who gets me things.

SEVENLY: Midge.

MIDGE: Come back tomorrow. We'll talk about it tomorrow.

SEVENLY: I can't get away from the house.

MIDGE: You got away from the house tonight.

SEVENLY: Everybody's asleep.

MIDGE: Then come back when everybody's asleep, I mean, fuck, this isn't rocket science. Go home. Come back tomorrow. We'll talk about it tomorrow.

SEVENLY: Do you promise you won't say a word to anybody about this?

MIDGE: It would be very unprofessional for me to say a word to anybody about this.

SEVENLY: Okay. Okay. *(She puts her coat on, goes to the door.)*

MIDGE: But I've never been much of a professional.

(Pause)

SEVENLY: I think we should talk some more.

MIDGE: Oh, you want to talk more?

SEVENLY: I do, yes.

MIDGE: Okay. What would you like to talk about.

SEVENLY: What would *you* like to talk about? *(She stands with her mug, getting groggy.)*

MIDGE: *(Lulling, careful)* Have you been to the Wisconsin Dells? You should go. It's really close. Your kids will love it. It's like Las Vegas for Kids. Water parks. Go Karts. Bungee Jumping. Miniature Golf. The Wonder Spot. A futuristic house made entirely of Styrofoam. And: The Famous Wisconsin Dells Ducks. They're military vehicles that can go on land and water. They take you on a tour all over and there's this joke the driver says driving down the winding road with a steep drop off fenced by chicken wire. And the driver says, "if it can hold a chicken it can certainly hold a duck."

(MIDGE *kisses* SEVENLY *on the mouth.* SEVENLY *drops the mug, her legs go weak, limbs heavy, eyes bleary.* MIDGE *catches her.)*

SEVENLY: Oh my. Oh goodness.

MIDGE: You smell like soap.

(MIDGE *helps* SEVENLY *sit.)*

MIDGE: Told you it's good coffee. Two sugars.

SEVENLY: What's…

MIDGE: Sssshhh, relax. You'll get some good sleep now. I'll get you the thing you need. I'll take care of you. *(She touches* SEVENLY's *stomach.)* You don't have to have this baby if you don't want it. I do have one more secret. Haven't told anyone. Sevenly?

SEVENLY: …mm…

MIDGE: My father's not dead. Not really.

(Lights to black)

END OF ACT ONE

ACT TWO

Scene Four

(Early the next morning. SEVENLY *is sound asleep in the kitchen.* VALERIE *sits at the kitchen table, drinking coffee, working on the newspaper crossword. Pop music from a mix-tape plays on a tape recorder.)*

VALERIE: Actress Turner. ...Lana... Jai *blank*. J – A – I, then a blank, four letters. ...Don't worry yourself, I know it, I just thought you may want to chime in. Jai alai, in just about every morning's crossword being it's a boon for vowels, A –L – A – I, three out of four letters being vowels. Jai alai. Whatever that is. You know, I do these things every single morning and every single m—

*(*SEVENLY *wakes.)*

VALERIE: ...hello. Gail keeps at me for not locking my doors, so funny it's you the first break-in I have, though not the first time I greet the day to someone asleep here. Midge has this no-good acquaintance, Gordy Laroux, works at the Starbucks, found him strung out asleep right here on the kitchen table. He has a bit of a mouth on him. I was forced to go after that stubble-chinned candyass with my meat cleaver.

SEVENLY: What time is it?

VALERIE: Near five-thirty.

SEVENLY: In the morning?

VALERIE: In the morning. You must've had some night, huh, you weren't drinking were you?

SEVENLY: No. No. I need to get home before Donal and the kids wake up. They'll be expecting breakfast and...

VALERIE: Have a sit there, take it easy. Just sit a moment.... You wouldn't happen to know where Midge went, would you?

SEVENLY: No.

VALERIE: Her car's not here, thought that was a bit strange. Not like her to be the least bit productive before nine in the a.m. You see Midge earlier?

SEVENLY: Earlier?

VALERIE: Whenever you came in and before you conked out, you see my darling daughter Midge?

SEVENLY: I did, yes.

VALERIE: She didn't say where she was going?

SEVENLY: No.

VALERIE: Will she be back?

SEVENLY: I don't know.

VALERIE: Seems you two had a little talk over coffee last night or such.

SEVENLY: How—did you know?

VALERIE: Coffee mugs out, I saw.

SEVENLY: Ohh.

VALERIE: It's just not like her to take off. You know? Midge doesn't take off, she's very stagnant, like a pond. It's one thing Midge doesn't come home at night, because that's failure to return. Another thing entirely to be here one night then not the next morning because you know what that is? Success in leaving. I can make you some breakfast. Toast?

SEVENLY: No, thank you.

VALERIE: You sure now? Donal is worried about you. Seems to think something's wrong. Now you don't have to tell me anything, but if there happens to be something on your mind, well. Here I am. Somebody to talk to. I am a good listener, you know.

SEVENLY: Thank you, Valerie, but—

VALERIE: But you need to go home, okay then. Out of curiosity, because I know Midge isn't a social creature, you mind telling me what you talked about? She happen to say anything about her father?

SEVENLY: She...may have. I can't really...recall what she said.

VALERIE: You must've been tuckered out.

SEVENLY: I should go.

VALERIE: My door is open and unlocked if you ever need to talk about the baby.

(SEVENLY *halts.*)

(VALERIE *claps her hands*) I knew it, dang I'm good! I'm right, right. Right? I am right, aren't I, you're going to have a baby?

(GAIL *enters the kitchen. She's dressed in most of her cop uniform for the cold weather—hat, gloves, boots—but she's not wearing a coat and her shirt is sweat through. She's high on Crystal Meth. She'll root through the cabinets, drawers and get cereal and a bowl and spoon*)

GAIL: So, ah. This waitress. Um. (*Laughs*) Some waitress. SallyShirleySusie some "s" name some name starting with "s". Sssssandra? This waitress. Works at the Blue Squirrel you ever been to The Blue Squirrel the bar slash restaurant though it's not a *restaurant* restaurant they just serve buffalo wings on Friday night. You can throw your peanut shells on the floor do you like peanuts? Do you like peanuts?

SEVENLY: Peanuts are all right.

VALERIE: What in the blast is wrong with you?

GAIL: What in the blast is wrong with me what in the blast is wrong with *you!*

VALERIE: Where's your coat. It's freezing outside.

GAIL: I'm hhhhhot. I'm burning up. Here I'll show ya. *(Gets a meat thermometer from the drawer and sticks it in her mouth)* Check it out. Check out how hot I am. Feel my pulse. No really feel my pulse. My heart's gonna explode.

VALERIE: Are you on drugs?

GAIL: Am I on what?

VALERIE: Drugs.

GAIL: *(Nervous laugh)* Look. Look. Okay, look, okay. Look. Okay. Look. If I don't know, ah. The baseline of narcotics, the, you know, what the kids are using, what good am I? If I don't know these things, these things we confiscate? Signs to look for in an individual who may be using such and such this, or such and such that. If I don't know these things intimately, personally, well. What good am I? I want to be the best police officer I can be. I have to know things.

VALERIE: What are you on?

GAIL: Nothing. Crystal Meth.

SEVENLY: What's Crystal Meth?

GAIL: I run the D.A.R.E. program at the elementary school. Dare to keep kids off drugs, lemme know if you ever want me to have a chat with your kids. Me n McGruff the Crime Dog are like THIS: *(Crosses fingers. Then dead serious:)* It's just a guy in a dog suit.

(GAIL *starts doing the crossword*)

VALERIE: Gail.

GAIL: If you don't like peanuts, there's popcorn, which you can also throw on the floor I imagine, but, like, why would you do that? Why throw perfectly good popcorn on the floor. Why? I don't recommend eating the popcorn. I do not think they wash those popcorn baskets. I do not think those popcorn baskets are very sanitary.

VALERIE: That's not tic-tac-toe, that's a crossword puzzle.

(GAIL *throws the paper and pen aside.*)

VALERIE: I think you ought to go home.

GAIL: I can't go home. That slut is in my home. That shit eating taint licking cocksucking slut is in my home that SallyShirleySusie with my husband and the two of them have the the the *audacity* to do it in my marriage bed.

VALERIE: This isn't the first time this has happened, Gail.

GAIL: No but by god it's the last time! (*She checks her gun.*)

VALERIE: Why don't you leave the gun here?

GAIL: I'm supposed to have my gun, Valerie, I'm supposed to have Rosalinda with me at all times. At all times! I am supposed to have Rosalinda with me *at all times.*

VALERIE: Sure but are you supposed to use Rosalinda for shooting husband-stealing sluts? Is that what the department issued her for. Yes or no.

GAIL: Yes?

VALERIE: No.

GAIL: No.

VALERIE: They did not issue your gun for shooting husband-stealing sluts. They issued it for other things.

GAIL: I shot that coyote in your backyard that one Thanksgiving.

VALERIE: I know, you did. And that wasn't a coyote but Midge's dog Steve, so give me the gun before you hurt someone.

GAIL: No. No way, no hoo—how. Hoo how.

VALERIE: If you won't give it to me, let Sevenly take it from you.

SEVENLY: Guns make me feel very uneasy, Valerie.

VALERIE: I don't like guns either and I'm not asking you to use it. Just take it from Gail and set it down over there. You'll give it to Sevenly, won't you?

GAIL: Sure, yeah, sure. I'll give it to Sevenly, I'll give it to her. Come and get it.

(SEVENLY *approaches.* GAIL *jabs the gun in* SEVENLY's *stomach.*)

GAIL: I'm just messin.

(GAIL *holds the gun in her palm for* SEVENLY *to take.* SEVENLY *takes the gun.* VALERIE *takes* GAIL *by the hair and wrenches her head back.*)

VALERIE: I am sorry for the way Eddie treats you, but you win little sympathy from me when you go all freewheeling with your firearms, pointing your gun like that when she's going to be having a baby.

GAIL: Ohh congratulations a baaaaybe, just what the world needs another baaaay—

(VALERIE *gives* GAIL's *hair a tugging twist.*)

GAIL: —hey!

SEVENLY: I'm. Not.

VALERIE: You said you were having a baby.

SEVENLY: You implied I was.

VALERIE: Oh. Well. It's just that Donal is worried about you, and. I thought, maybe that was a good guess being so fertile the way you are. It's not at all because I think you're fat.

SEVENLY: You think I'm fat?

VALERIE: No no no, you have a respectable figure, it's just that maybe I thought you were walking a little funny.

SEVENLY: You think I walk funny?

GAIL: I remember a time when you didn't have your hand in my hair, those were nice times.

VALERIE: Apologize to your sister-in-law for pointing your gun, and pray to whatever you need to pray to that she learns to tolerate you as much as I've tolerated you all these years.

GAIL: Yeah right.

(VALERIE *twists* GAIL's *hair.*)

GAIL: Ow. Sorry.

VALERIE: To her.

GAIL: You got my head wrenched back I can't exactly direct my apologies to anything but the cracked plaster in your dumb ceiling, you called me an idiot, well who's the idiot now—

(VALERIE *twists* GAIL's *hair.*)

GAIL: —ow! Is all I'm sayin is who's the idiot now—

(VALERIE *twists.*)

GAIL: —ow! I'm just sayin—

(VALERIE *twists.*)

GAIL: —ow!

(VALERIE *directs* GAIL's *head toward* SEVENLY.)

GAIL: I'm sorry.

VALERIE: Go soak your head in the shower.

(VALERIE *releases* GAIL.)

GAIL: You're crazy, Valerie. I'm calling the cops.

VALERIE: You *are* the cops.

GAIL: Well good! I'm glad I know about this! (*She exits, immediately reenters.*) Going to grab my cereal I'm super hungry.

VALERIE: Grab your cereal.

GAIL: I'm super hungry.

VALERIE: I've heard that rumor.

GAIL: Who told you that???

VALERIE: Get what you need to get.

(GAIL *gets her cereal, opens the fridge, grabs the milk. There's only a splash left. She shakes it, then chucks it across the kitchen.*)

GAIL: What am I supposed to do, eat this raw?

VALERIE: Do what you want.

GAIL: "Do what you want." Do what I want, I *will* do what I want. (*Stands there*)

VALERIE: Well?

GAIL: I'm overwhelmed by the possibilities.

VALERIE: How about you pick up that flung milk gallon and put it back from whence it came.

(GAIL *does so, and looks through the fridge.*)

VALERIE: Donal said he was worried about you and I assumed unrightly about what it was was bothering you. If the implication upset you, I apologize. It would

be nice if we could be neighborly like. I'm not saying
we *have* to. But if it's something we could work on, it
might be nice to have a, you know, a...

SEVENLY: Friend?

VALERIE: Sure. One of those. And I don't at all think
you're fat.

(GAIL *takes the milk gallon—the one filled with blood—from
the fridge and pours it on her cereal and eats.* SEVENLY
notices the peculiarity, but VALERIE'*s back is to it.*)

SEVENLY: Do you keep milk containers of blood in your
refrigerator?

VALERIE: Sometimes, yes, don't you? One moment.
Gail.

GAIL: What?

VALERIE: Probably don't want to be drinking that milk,
Gail.

GAIL: What?

VALERIE: That funny-looking milk, Gail, probably don't
want to be drinking that, it's going to taste as funny as
it looks. ...Gail!

GAIL: What?

VALERIE: Excuse me.

(VALERIE *grabs the bloody gallon, trailed by* GAIL *who has
blood dripping down her chin.*)

VALERIE: Sit.

GAIL: But—

VALERIE: Sit.

GAIL: No, but—

VALERIE: *Sit!*

GAIL: I'm going to sit but not because you say so. (*Sits*)

VALERIE: This is blood.

GAIL: Well that's nuts.

VALERIE: Sit there. Relax.

(GAIL *sits, still, relaxing.*)

VALERIE: Okay? Good. *(She wipes the blood off* GAIL's *face.)* What I'm understanding is that you're a little vague about last night, am I right?

GAIL: I'm kinda vague about last night too.

VALERIE: I'm really not talking to you.

SEVENLY: There are certain vague parts.

VALERIE: Let me help you suss out your memory here. What's the last thing you remember talking about.

SEVENLY: The Wisconsin Dells. The Ducks.

VALERIE: The Ducks. That it? You can't remember what she said about Frank.

SEVENLY: Why do you want to know?

(MIDGE *enters from outside. She has a pharmacy bag.* GAIL *approaches her.)*

GAIL: Hey do you have Gordy's number, phone number?

MIDGE: What's wrong with you?

GAIL: Nothing nothing.

VALERIE: Seems she got into some Meth.

MIDGE: Did you confiscate meth from Gordy? That stuff's really not good for you. His recipe is wacky. *(To* SEVENLY*)* You okay? You wanna, uh. Meet me later.

VALERIE: Meet you later, you two are buddies now?

MIDGE: Yeah.

VALERIE: What have you been talking about.

MIDGE: We're just…friends. Right?

VALERIE: Seems you had an interesting conversation last night?

MIDGE: I thought we were keeping all that about the baby between me and you?

GAIL: *(Finally figuring it out)* Ohhhhhh.

VALERIE: Gail, why don't you go lay down in my bedroom. Have a shower, lay down a bit, okay?

GAIL: *(To* SEVENLY*)* You're a liar. *(She exits.)*

VALERIE: Suppose you haven't told Donal about the baby.

MIDGE: Mom, don't...

VALERIE: It's none of my business, is it.

MIDGE: Well, okay. Good.

*(*VALERIE *grabs the pharmacy bag from* MIDGE.*)*

MIDGE: Give that back.

VALERIE: You can't be feeding her drugs if she's going to have a baby. Sevenly, don't get mixed up in things like this.

MIDGE: Give me the bag. Mom. I'm warning you.

VALERIE: You're warning me?

MIDGE: I am.

VALERIE: You're warning me, oh, okay, I can see you've got your "I'm warning you face" on you, sure.

MIDGE: I'm going to count to three. One. Two. Three. ...Four... Don't make me count five, Mom.

*(*SEVENLY, *with* GAIL's *gun:)*

SEVENLY: Would you please give me the bag please!

(Pause)

MIDGE: Here, Sevenly, give me the g—

SEVENLY: Sit down. Both of you.

(*They do*)

SEVENLY: What did you put in my coffee last night?

VALERIE: Midge, did you drug Sevenly? How many times have I told you not to do that to guests?

MIDGE: You don't mind when I do it to Uncle Eddie.

VALERIE: Eddie doesn't count. He's at his best when he's unconscious.

MIDGE: I just gave her something to help her sleep some. Doesn't she look less tired?

VALERIE: You do look fresh.

MIDGE: I wanted you to not feel so bad.

SEVENLY: Give me the bag.

VALERIE: Sevenly, drugs aren't the answer. I don't know if you watch *20/20*.

MIDGE: Your notions concerning pharmaceuticals are antique so I'll forgive you your *faux pas*.

VALERIE: *Faux pas*.

MIDGE: It's French.

VALERIE: For?

MIDGE: It's just French—god—can't I say something French without you being all up in my grill?

SEVENLY: Give me the bag!!!

VALERIE: What sort of drug is this?

SEVENLY: We all have big families. Lots of children. It's just how it is, it's what's expected. Our faith. Our faith in God. I love my children, I love them dearly. Please understand that.

I have four sisters, two brothers. I'm the youngest in my family. Five years ago my oldest sister Susan died

giving birth to her seventh child. Four years ago my
second oldest sister Helen died giving birth to her
seventh child. Three years ago my third oldest sister
Debra died giving birth to her seventh child.
I was my mother's seventh child. My name was chosen
in a resigned sigh. My name was chosen in the way
you chose the wood finish of your own casket. There
is no number beyond seven. It's something else.
Something bigger that's striking us down. And if it's
God, why would he do that to us? Why?
This will be my seventh child. I have to do something.
Now. Give me the bag.

(VALERIE *doesn't release the bag.* SEVENLY *puts the gun to*
MIDGE's *head.)*

MIDGE: Mom?

(VALERIE *gives up the bag to* SEVENLY. SEVENLY *puts down*
the gun, takes her brownie pan, and exits.)

VALERIE: Go check on your Aunt Gail.

(MIDGE *exits.* VALERIE *goes to the phone, dials.)*

VALERIE: Donal? Hi, it's Valerie. You're sure right to be
worried about your wife.

Scene Five

(Late that night. GAIL *at the kitchen table with a tape*
recorder and gun.)

GAIL: *(Hits "record" button)* Okay. Hey. If my
handwriting weren't all chicken scratch I'd leave a note
but, uh. Crud. That's stupid. *(Stop, rewind, record)* Hi.
This is Gail. Um. If you're listening to this, it means,
um. y'know, I'm probably dead. On the floor. Or
something. No. *(Stop, rewind. record)* Hi. Um. Blehhh.
Poop. *(Stop, rewind, record)* Let's see, uh. Hi. Gail here.
These are my last words. Um, first to Eddie. You're a

bastard for sleeping around with cocktail waitresses
that Shirley or Susie or Sally. I let you follow your
dreams and you didn't give two halfshits about my
dreams and I had dreams, whole dreams, not just
halfshits of dreams, and you better believe I would not
have encouraged your baseball dream had I known the
steroids would squash your little sperms. To Valerie.
You were never good enough for my brother and if
you didn't kill him then you drove him to it and that's
all I have to say about that. Though you do bring me
good cuts of meat and you don't make me pay for
them. So, thanks. Midge, you irritate me. A lot. But I
know how much you like Billy Joel so you can have my
records Glass Houses and 52nd Street. You're welcome
to Piano Man, but it has a big scratch. And, also, have
my collection of souvenir ashtrays, I've collected one
from every state except Montana and Hawaii. And
Delaware but… *(Scoffs)* Sevenly, if you want my Peter
Paul & Mary record your kids might like that, it's very
wholesome. Donal: I don't have anything for you. You
made fun of me when we were younger and you made
me feel stupid and you set my teddy bear on fire. It's
you who should've died instead of Frank. Donal and
Valerie, if you thought I was blind to your repugnant
behavior together, well, I assure you, I know far more
than you ever suspected.
And if the lot of you think I haven't been very nice,
then that's just the way I am and what I felt is what I
felt and I can't change things now. The Crystal Meth
I did gave me clarity and perspective, mostly on the
ineffectiveness and wrong-headedness of our school
district's anti-drug programs. *(Pause)* I loved Frank
and I miss him. I miss him so much. The other day, I
drove to the lake, late, and the lake, it was frozen, and
out there, I thought I saw Frank give me a wave before
going under. It was my imagination I suppose. I'll have
to live and die with that I suppose. And.... Despite all

the stuff I've said, I love most of you some[ ] some reason. That's it. Goodbye.

(Stop. Pause. Rewind. Play)

TAPE RECORDER: "Let's see, uh. Hi. Gail here. These a[ ] my last words. Um, first to Eddie. You're a —" *(Tape abruptly cuts to a pop song)*

GAIL: Aww noooo. No no no no no no no! You didn't record any of that! My final words are lost! …You know what? Fine. This is good. I'm glad you didn't get that. *(She stops the tape.)* Here are my final words that nobody will hear: I'm going to kill myself and nobody is going to know why. This'll be just one more mystery. *(She puts the gun under her chin and pulls the trigger. Click—empty. She tries again. Empty chamber. She puts the gun to her head and is about to pull the trigger)*

MIDGE: Bang. *(She enters, having been lurking the whole time.)*

GAIL: You weren't going to stop me from killing myself?

MIDGE: What about your Billy Joel records?

GAIL: What *about* my Billy Joel records.

MIDGE: You said I could have them.

GAIL: I said that when I thought I was going to be dead.

MIDGE: Right.

GAIL: And I'd have no use for them anymore.

MIDGE: Right.

GAIL: But I'm not dead so you see what I'm getting at? I'm alive and I still like Billy Joel so you can't have my Billy Joel records.

MIDGE: Not even Piano Man with the scratch?

GAIL: Not even Piano Man with the scratch and the fact that I want Piano Man, scratch and all, is a testament to Billy Joel's talent.

MIDGE: What about the ashtrays?

GAIL: Are you thick? I'm not dead!

MIDGE: So?

GAIL: So *no*. I have a duplicate Indiana, you can have Indiana.

MIDGE: I don't want Indiana.

GAIL: Well who does? What do you want?

MIDGE: New Hampshire.

GAIL: Get outta here. Go to bed. Look, I'm fine. I'm not going to do anything. I was in a bad way before. I feel better now. Like I needed to cleanse myself of that. You know? I don't know what got into me. Like that was a sign. That my gun didn't go off.

(MIDGE *opens the chamber and empties the contents of the gun on the table...jelly beans*)

GAIL: That's real good of you taking the bullets out of my gun. I'm rather fond of my brain, and I'm glad it's not all over the ceiling. You're my brother's daughter and I've treated you like just another no-good pistol whipped kid in the back of my squad car. I owe you an apology if you think I've been too hard on you.

MIDGE: That's nice of you, Aunt Gail.

GAIL: Apology accepted?

MIDGE: Yeah, yeah, apology accepted.

GAIL: Good. Great. Also owe you an apology for shooting your dog.

(MIDGE *tenses, shocked, angry. Stares at* GAIL)

Okay, here's what happened. It was Thanksgiving at
your house, and you were at work, and I thought there
was a coyote in the backyard. But after a six-pack of
Milwaukee's Best, pretty much everything looks like
a coyote. I feel so much better telling you this! Like a
two-ton weight's been lifted off my shoulders! Phew!
...Midge? Now you're not mad, are you? I'm real
sorry. I thought it would be better you thinking that he
just ran off in the woods or something. No?

MIDGE: I would rather've known the truth.

GAIL: Is there anything I can do to make you feel
better? (Pause. She takes off one of her socks, puts it on
her hand as a sock puppet:) "Hello, Midge. Do you like
cheese?"

(MIDGE stares at GAIL. Then snorts a stifled laugh through
her nose.)

GAIL: See, everybody likes sock puppets.

MIDGE: Nobody likes sock puppets.

GAIL: But you're smiling now, so, that's something.
That's something, at least. Steve was a good dog, and it
was quick and painless. Probably. You ever do Meth?

MIDGE: Why?

GAIL: You wanna get high with me sometime, that
might be fun. Something we can do together, like
family bonding.

MIDGE: I don't do drugs.

GAIL: Well that strikes me as a bit hypocritical.

MIDGE: Do you know how dangerous Meth is?

GAIL: I am an officer of the law. I // run the D.A.R.E.
program.

MIDGE: (Overlap) You run the D.A.R.E. program, yeah
yeah yeah.

GAIL: You got anymore stuff in your stuff, (MIDGE's *backpack*) fun stuff, just, you know, for fun and laughs. The night is young.

MIDGE: You should lay off the junk, Aunt Gail. I don't want to be the reason you don't wake up in the morning.

GAIL: Only person ever seemed to care about me was Frank. And he's gone. Least I know you inherited some of his goodness. You wouldn't happen to have any extra of those pills your mom takes to sleep? A quick, sound sleep would be a comfort.

(MIDGE *gets a bottle of pills.*)

MIDGE: What do you know about my mom and Donal.

GAIL: Valerie and Donal.

MIDGE: "Repugnant behavior."

GAIL: *(Pause, uncomfortable)* What do you want to know?

MIDGE: Everything.

Scene Six

(Next morning. VALERIE *at the kitchen table, newspaper, coffee.* GAIL *has her head down in her arms, asleep on the table.* VALERIE *rewinds the tape in the tape recorder, presses play.)*

TAPE RECORDER: "Let's see, uh. Hi. Gail here. These are my last words. Um, first to Eddie. You're a—" *(Tape abruptly cuts to a pop song.)*

*(*VALERIE *stops the tape.)*

VALERIE: That was my favorite mix tape.

*(*MIDGE *enters, beginning her breakfast routine.)*

MIDGE: Can you be honest with me, Mom?

VALERIE: I've always said, honesty is best.

MIDGE: You've never always said that.

VALERIE: I've sometimes thought that's something I should've always said. That would've been a good something to always say. If I'm going to be honest with you Midge, I think if you ever want to find // a decent man you need to make the effort.

MIDGE: (//Overlap) Ohhhhhh stop, just stop, stop talking, god.

VALERIE: I'll be damned if I see you spend the rest of your life alone. Maybe you'll get the inspiration to find a knot to tie yourself after you go to that retarded boy's wedding.

MIDGE: He didn't invite me.

VALERIE: You can probably go anyway.

MIDGE: But I didn't get an invitation.

VALERIE: What's he going to do, kick you out? He's retarded.

(DONAL enters with SEVENLY.)

DONAL: Did you give my wife some illicit pharmaceuticals? Valerie called, told me you may have given her some pills.

(MIDGE looks at VALERIE.)

VALERIE: You know how I feel about it. I can't just stand by let something like this happen.

DONAL: I don't know who you think you are or what you said to my wife to make her consider this as an option. You are never to speak to her again. Do you understand?

MIDGE: (To SEVENLY) Did you take any?

DONAL: Was I unclear, the part where I said you're never to speak to her?

(MIDGE *looks at* SEVENLY, SEVENLY *looks away.* MIDGE *gets up.*)

DONAL: I'm not done talking to you, you stay right here.

MIDGE: Oh, who are you now? My dad?

DONAL: You let this happen in your own house?

VALERIE: I was asleep when it happened. Seems to me you don't communicate so well with your wife there.

DONAL: We communicate just fine.

VALERIE: If that were so I don't think you'd have to ask me to act the spy.

DONAL: What all went on here behind my back?

SEVENLY: Donal, I asked her for help.

DONAL: You don't need her help.

SEVENLY: You know what happened to my sisters…

DONAL: What happened to your sisters is not going to happen to you.

SEVENLY: How can you know?

DONAL: Because it's not going to happen. It's not. You're nervous. You were nervous with the other six, remember how nervous you were? *She* can't help you.

SEVENLY: You're wrong.

DONAL: I'm not.

(GAIL *falls out of her chair, passed out on the floor. Everybody looks at her.*)

MIDGE: Maybe she took something.

VALERIE: Oh *maybe* you think? What did she take?

(DONAL *attends to* GAIL.)

DONAL: *(To* MIDGE*)* This is your doing?

MIDGE: I told her not to do anything. She got into my stuff.

DONAL: Face down on your kitchen table and you don't do anything?

VALERIE: She was face down and she groaned a bit, and that's not far different from her usual demeanor.

DONAL: Gail? Wake up.

GAIL: *(Wakes)* Mm. Frank?

DONAL: No, I'm not Frank. ...Gail? ...Gail!

SEVENLY: She needs to go to the hospital.

DONAL: What did she take? Midge, what did she take.

MIDGE: Sleeping pills. Same stuff you use to help you sleep.

VALERIE: Oh geez, how many did she take?

MIDGE: Enough to kill her.

DONAL: Come on, give me a hand here. Valerie, help, please. Help me get her to the car.

VALERIE: 'Course.

DONAL: Jesus, this unbelievable.

(VALERIE and DONAL exit with GAIL.)

SEVENLY: He flushed the pills in the toilet.

MIDGE: What do you want me to do?

SEVENLY: Get me more.

MIDGE: I'll get you the phone and address of a doctor. He'll take good care of you. It's the best way.

SEVENLY: Will you go with me?

MIDGE: Thought you didn't want to go anywhere with me.

SEVENLY: I need somebody there. You're the only one.

MIDGE: Really? Of course I'll go with you if you—

(DONAL *enters*. SEVENLY *moves away from* MIDGE)

DONAL: Valerie went on ahead with Gail, we'll meet her there. Let's go.

SEVENLY: Donal, the kids.

DONAL: What ab—okay—mm—you'll have to go home then. I'll call you from the hospital, let you know.

SEVENLY: Okay.

DONAL: It'll be all right. Go on home. I'll call soon.

(SEVENLY *looks to* MIDGE.)

DONAL: I said go home.

(SEVENLY *exits.* DONAL *reaches into his coat, pulls out a check book, and writes her a check.*)

DONAL: Your mother and father may have turned a blind eye to your wicked behavior, but I will not. My wife is upset and fragile and confused. My sister clearly has emotional problems and you shove pills down her throat. Who do you think you are you can do this. Who do you think are? (*Hands the check to* MIDGE) That should cover your expenses well enough.

MIDGE: Expenses for what?

DONAL: I want you to go away and that will cover your expenses for travel, living, anywhere, anywhere other than Baraboo. Fold that up, take it to the bank. You need more, give me a call. I'll send you more on the condition you don't set one toe back here.

MIDGE: This is a lot of money.

DONAL: It is, yes.

MIDGE: If I take this and use it to get a boob job, you'd keep sending me more as long as I don't come back?

DONAL: I don't think you need one of those.

MIDGE: You checking out my rack?

DONAL: No.

MIDGE: Yeah you were.

DONAL: I was not.

MIDGE: You totally were checking out my rack.

DONAL: There was no rack-checking-outing going on. Now take the money, Midge. Go, and don't ever come back. *(Pause)* Are you crying?

MIDGE: I'm not crying.

DONAL: You don't need to be having a bit of a cry.

MIDGE: I'm not having a bit of a cry.

DONAL: Oh you're not, now? Then what's that leaking out of your eyes and your nose?

MIDGE: Tears and snot.

DONAL: *(Fatherly)* Tears and snot, ohh, well, tears and snot. If that's not the recipe for a bit of a cry I don't know what is. Here now. Here. *(Holding out a tissue)*

MIDGE: No.

DONAL: Take it.

MIDGE: I don't want your stupid Kleenex and I don't want your stupid money. You're gonna need it for your wife's funeral when she has your stupid seventh baby. *(She slams the check down on the table.)* But you can't watch her all the time, can you? Who knows where she'll go next.

(DONAL hands MIDGE a tissue. She dabs her eyes, wipes her nose.)

DONAL: Stay away from her. I meant what I said, I don't want you speaking to her.

MIDGE: She's lonely. She's scared. Round here, lonely and scared people have a habit of disappearing.

DONAL: Is that so?

MIDGE: Unfortunately.

DONAL: What lonely and scared people have disappeared? *(Pause)* Do you know something about what happened to your father?

MIDGE: My who?

DONAL: Don't—Midge—I'm through playing games, you understand me now? What happened to Frank. *(He grabs her arm, hard.)* Did you do something to him?

MIDGE: *(Shakes him off)* Don't touch me! Don't.

DONAL: Please, just, Midge.

MIDGE: Wasn't me did anything. He and mom had a fight and he left for the lake. He couldn't stay here anymore, knowing the truth. Was real low what mom said to him. He wasn't strong enough for truth.

DONAL: What did your mother tell him.

(Pause)

MIDGE: Is it true?

(Pause)

DONAL: You're Frank's girl, that's that. We are not speaking of this ever again. Understand?

MIDGE: Fine.

DONAL: You're Frank's girl. Okay?

MIDGE: Okay.

DONAL: This is what drove him out to the lake that night, hearing that?

MIDGE: No, that didn't drive him out there. Was me drove him out there. In my car. He needed a ride, couldn't get his car started.

DONAL: You were with him that night.

MIDGE: Yeah.

DONAL: What were you doing out there?

MIDGE: Fishin'. I got cold. Went home. Left him out there. And he never came home.

DONAL: You just left him out there on the lake?

MIDGE: He wanted me to go away.

DONAL: Is that the truth. You left him out there and he never came home?

(Pause)

MIDGE: I can show you where he *was*. Where I left him, on the lake. Would you like that? If I showed you where I left him?

DONAL: All right. Show me where you left him.

MIDGE: It's cold out there, you know. Always colder that you expect. Bundle up.

DONAL: I'll meet you outside.

(DONAL exits. MIDGE puts on her coat, picks up VALERIE's meat cleaver, and exits.)

Scene Seven

(The next morning. VALERIE at the kitchen table. MIDGE enters, breakfast routine. She's limping on a sprained ankle.)

VALERIE: Gave a call over to the hospital this morning, Eddie says your aunt is doing fine today, just fine. Eddie was worried about her. Nothing like a near fatal overdose to keep a marriage together. *(Pause)* Funny that Donal didn't show at the hospital. Or last night. Or this morning, for that matter.

MIDGE: That's weird.

VALERIE: Wonder what happened to him.

MIDGE: He didn't show up this morning?

VALERIE: No.

MIDGE: Yeah that's weird.

VALERIE: Is weird, isn't it. Also called Sevenly. She's a bit distraught.

MIDGE: Oh yeah?

VALERIE: Husband up and vanished, of course she's upset.

MIDGE: I have to get ready for work.

VALERIE: You seem a bit gimpy this morning, sweetheart. Why don't you have a seat. What's the matter with your foot?

MIDGE: I sprained it.

VALERIE: Doing what? *(Pause)* Remember when you were a little girl and you had that subscription to Highlights Magazine for Children. You remember that, Highlights Magazine...

MIDGE: Yeah, yeah.

VALERIE: And in every issue they had that "What's Wrong With This Picture?" game and there was, oh, a dog with a boot on his head or the sun outside the kitchen window was square or maybe it was, instead of square, it was purple, a purple sun, or something, right? And you had to stare at this picture. Had to figure out what was wrong with it, circle all the things that were wrong with a particular domestic scene. Is this ringing a bell or am I just talking...

MIDGE: Yeah, yeah.

VALERIE: Highlights Magazine, very educational, okay. Well. What's wrong with this picture, Midge?

MIDGE: What picture?

(VALERIE gestures indicating the entire kitchen.)

MIDGE: I don't know.

VALERIE: You didn't even try. *(She draws a circle in the air around her cleaver in the butcher block)* You don't see what's wrong with this here? How bout now? How bout now? Now? If I keep circling you think you may get it? ...A little ding in the blade that I know was not there yesterday. I can account for all the other dings in my cutlery, but this teeny tiny little ding is not one I can account for.

MIDGE: You account for your dings?

VALERIE: Mm hm.

(MIDGE stands.)

VALERIE: Sit.

MIDGE: I dropped it, I dropped your meat cleaver, I'm sorry, okay. Sorry.

VALERIE: When did you drop it?

MIDGE: When I was running through the woods.

VALERIE: Okay, let's go back, because I'm running into a little problem with your story-telling here. What I understand is—and feel free to jump in, help me fill out the details where you can—While I was at the hospital with your aunt—

MIDGE: Aunt Gail.

VALERIE: Really don't need help with the obvious stuff.

MIDGE: Fine.

VALERIE: While I was at the hospital—

MIDGE: Don't need my help, fine.

VALERIE: Are you done? At the hospital, with your aunt who overdosed on pills you let into this house.

MIDGE: I didn't force Aunt Gail to do anything.

VALERIE: But you enabled her, isn't that so. You're an enabler as John Stossel would say.

MIDGE: Is it my problem she's inherently flawed?

VALERIE: No, it's not, but it's your problem she's going to stay that way, and I have an idea that maybe you weren't running through the woods for exercise. Why did you bring my meat cleaver to the woods?

MIDGE: For protection. Out in the woods. I knew I'd be coming back alone, again.

VALERIE: Well the woods can be scary, sure. Whatever you have to do to feel safe, I understand.

MIDGE: You're not mad I took your cleaver?

VALERIE: No, 'course not.

MIDGE: But I dinged it.

VALERIE: Accidents happen. Just, in the future, please ask me if you'd like to borrow my cutlery, all right?

MIDGE: All right.

(VALERIE *hits* MIDGE *with a stunning blow upside the head with a coffee mug.*)

MIDGE: AAAAAOOOW!!! OW! FUCK!

VALERIE: That always works in the movies, I don't understand. (*She grabs* MIDGE *by the neck and wrangles her in a sleeper choke hold to compress the carotid artery and black her out.*) Did you see in the paper this morning, City Council voted to abolish the beer tent at the Old Fashioned Days Festival. Didn't I say that was going to happen sooner or later, because it's a family event? You said it wasn't going to happen, but from my mouth to God's ear.

(MIDGE *goes limp.*)

VALERIE: …I'm sorry, sweetheart, just a bit of necessary prep work.

MIDGE: *(Wakes)* What the fu—?

(VALERIE slams MIDGE's head on the table, and pushes her on top of the table. MIDGE is finally unconscious. VALERIE ties MIDGE's feet with her robe tie. SEVENLY enters with her brownie pan.)

SEVENLY: Valerie, have you heard from D…?

VALERIE: Oh! She's fine. Midge has these spells. Are those more brownies for us?

SEVENLY: I had leftovers.

VALERIE: That's really nice, I've never had a next-door neighbor as nice as you before.

SEVENLY: Why are you doing that?

VALERIE: She'll be wily and I don't want her hurting herself. Really, it's for her own safety and comfort.

(SEVENLY helps VALERIE lift MIDGE onto the table and will hog-tie her.)

SEVENLY: Have you heard from Donal yet?

VALERIE: Mm, no.

SEVENLY: This isn't like him at all.

VALERIE: Disappearing on you.

SEVENLY: He wouldn't just…not come home. He wouldn't just not call me, even going to be the least bit late. I should call someone but the only other person I know is Gail in the hospital and—well unless that's where Donal went this morning, do you think that's where he is?

VALERIE: There's an off chance that Donal may not be coming back.

SEVENLY: What are you talking about?

VALERIE: Well…things happen. You know?

SEVENLY: No, Valerie, I don't know, what are you talking about?

VALERIE: The way it was with Frank is…was a couple days before we all figure out what happened. So you think maybe he's just…out. Until he's not just "out" but gone. Gone. You start thinking thoughts you'd never thought you'd think. The things you'd miss if he didn't come walking through that door like he did day after day. Like Frank could grill a good steak. Always said it was because the quality cuts I brought home from the shop, but I could grill that same exact meat and it would taste like shoe. Frank could probably grill a shoe and make it taste like filet mignon. I don't know how he did it. He was a vegetarian. Such is a person's contradictory nature.

SEVENLY: Valerie, where's my husband?

VALERIE: Midge knows the answer to that question. I'm glad you dropped by. Gimme one sec, I'll be right back.

(VALERIE *grabs her cleaver and exits.* SEVENLY *looks at* MIDGE, *brushes back* MIDGE's *hair to see the coffee mug welt.*)

MIDGE: *(Wakes suddenly)* …the fuck just happened…? Wh—? Ohhh my fucking god my head. …You need to go away. Don't be here. This is gonna be bad. This is gonna be really bad. Um. Yeah, this is gonna be bad. But you could untie me first.

SEVENLY: Valerie said you know where Donal is.

MIDGE: Untie me and I'll tell you.

SEVENLY: Tell me and I'll untie you.

MIDGE: How bout instead of that, you untie me then I'll tell you.

SEVENLY: You already said that.

MIDGE: I know you don't like me but I'd do anything for you. Please. Help me. Please.

(SEVENLY *starts to untie* MIDGE.)

MIDGE: Hurry.

(VALERIE *enters with the book:* Goodnight, Moon. *She stands watching* SEVENLY *work at the difficult knots.*)

VALERIE: See, what I haven't mentioned yet is that Midge took Donal out to the lake. Little field trip to the lake. Just her, Donal, and my meat cleaver.

(SEVENLY *stops untying.*)

VALERIE: How bout you fill us in on the details.

MIDGE: I took him to the lake. I left him out there.

VALERIE: You didn't *just* leave him. I know you did something to him.

MIDGE: How do you know that?

VALERIE: I know you, Midge. I'm your mother and I know you best. You did something to him. *(She pulls out* DONAL'*s check, shows* MIDGE.*)* Found this on the table. You want to tell me why Donal wrote you a check for a large sum of money?

MIDGE: He wanted me to go away.

VALERIE: Uh huh.

MIDGE: He did, he wanted me to go away so he wrote me a check.

VALERIE: Uh huh.

MIDGE: It's the truth!

VALERIE: But you're here...and Donal is not...which seems contrary to that truth. Sevenly? What do you think?

SEVENLY: It seems contrary.

MIDGE: Well sorry if it seems odd.

VALERIE: Well sorry you're gonna look odd if I tear one of your ear flaps off the side of your head.

(VALERIE *twists one of* MIDGE's *ears.*)

MIDGE: Gaaaahhhhhh!!! Stop!!!

(VALERIE *stops*)

VALERIE: I'm just noting this morning felt familiar, don't you think? Similar to a morning last year when your father didn't come home, don't you think? Am I having unreasonable thoughts or am I suffering a stunning case of déjà vu.

MIDGE: You think I killed dad?

VALERIE: I don't know, did you?

(MIDGE *shakes her head, sadly.*)

VALERIE: Suppose you didn't get a good look at the ding you left in my blade, but you see it there now, good and close. Riiiiight there. And you see how sharp this is too, dontchia? It would be one swift chop right here (MIDGE's *neck*) and maybe I'd have some peace to see the red cascade of you wash over the floor. Now what do you have to say to me about this (*The check*)

MIDGE: I like the way Donal signed the check. Me and him write with a similar lilt. Did you see the segment on *20/20* about how parents and kids often have similar handwriting?

(VALERIE *slams the book on the table.*)

VALERIE: How dare you imply that! How dare you! Frank adored you.

MIDGE: He could barely speak to me.

VALERIE: You answer me now: what did you do to Donal?

MIDGE: Would it make you feel better to hear I sunk your meat cleaver in his neck before I ran off? Fine. So I did.

(VALERIE *hands* Goodnight, Moon *to* SEVENLY.)

VALERIE: Looks like my little chicken may need some soothing from the chicken-reading expert. Was always Midge's favorite at bedtime. Start reading. ...Said start reading.

(SEVENLY *starts reading* Goodnight, Moon *out loud*)

VALERIE: Remember, now, when you were a little girl and you'd sometimes come to the butcher shop Saturdays to watch me chop chickens. And you asked where the went when they died? And I said they went to heaven. ...Just remember when you believed my stories with all your heart and you'll hardly feel the pain elsewhere. *(She holds* MIDGES *head down, cleaver at the ready.)* You tell me the truth now or this blade is going through your neck.

MIDGE: Was your fault he left, Mom! Was always your fault!

(VALERIE *raises the cleaver to chop* MIDGE's *neck, and* MIDGE *cries in terror. The kitchen door flies open and* DONAL *roars into the kitchen.* VALERIE *halts, stunned.* DONAL *is bundled up in scarf, hat, hood, obscured under layers, near frozen.)*

DONAL: Can't feel my hands. They're there, I know. I see them. But if I can't feel them it's like they're not even there. Feel my hands, please, feel them, tell me they're there.

(SEVENLY *squeezes* DONAL's *frozen hands. He yowls in pain. She lets go.)*

DONAL: No no don't stop it's all right. It's all right. I'm cold. It hurts.

SEVENLY: Where were you?!

DONAL: The lake! The woods! I was out there a long time searching! I thought maybe I could find my brother out there but I got lost. She left me and I got lost on the lake in the woods through the night. The only thing that kept my legs moving was you, thinking of you, getting back to you.

SEVENLY: I thought you were dead.

DONAL: I'm alive. My joints are burning. It's beautiful out there. The lake, at night. All those stars. Silent and cold and empty. *(He collapses on the floor.)*

SEVENLY: Donal!

DONAL: I thought I'd find him out there but there was nobody out there but me walking on the frozen water.

SEVENLY: Donal, please, get up.

DONAL: God I'm tired. I could sleep for a thousand days.

SEVENLY: Can you stand?

DONAL: I just want to sleep here.

SEVENLY: I'll get you home to bed. You're not sleeping on the floor.

DONAL: Sweetheart lemmie just take a nap.

SEVENLY: Come on.

DONAL: Just a quick nap.

SEVENLY: You're getting off the floor and getting home to bed. On your feet, soldier. Up. You made it this far, just a little bit further to bed. ...Donal! Get up!

(SEVENLY helps pull DONAL to his feet.)

SEVENLY: Are you steady?

DONAL: I'm okay. Yeah.

SEVENLY: Look, you're off the floor.

DONAL: I am, it's way down there now.

SEVENLY: Donal. Let's go home. We need to go.

DONAL: Forever?

SEVENLY: Come on.

DONAL: Oh god I love you. You're so beautiful.

SEVENLY: Time to go.

VALERIE: Don't go please don't go. I...

(DONAL *and* SEVENLY *exit.*)

MIDGE: You were gonna cut my fucking neck open.

(VALERIE *looks at the cleaver in her hand.* GAIL *enters.)*

GAIL: Eddie was asking about the t-bones again, and if you have any T-bones again... Something happen here?

MIDGE: Could you untie me please.

(GAIL *will untie* MIDGE.*)*

GAIL: Always getting yourself into some mess or other. Like that time you set your hair on fire making soup. Out of a can. Condensed. Anyway, I've been discharged from the hospital. Didn't overdose nearly enough for a longer stay according to my insurance policy. Hey, you hear me ask you about the meat?

VALERIE: Eddie, T-bones, yeah.

GAIL: *(To* MIDGE*)* I perhaps took a few too many of those sleeping pills against your professional advice, so. I will overlook your negligence in not removing them from my possession. Oh, Valerie, thanks for driving me to the hospital yesterday, I really appreciate that. I'd like to return the favor, so feel free to give me a call if you need a ride home from the hospital today.

VALERIE: A ride home from the hospital today?

GAIL: For the stitches.

VALERIE: For the stitches?

GAIL: For when I stuck you with my pocket knife.

VALERIE: For when you what?

(GAIL *sticks her pocket knife in* VALERIE'*s side*)

GAIL: Not so piss-ant now, eh?

VALERIE: You stabbed me!

GAIL: Ohhh is that what I did, 'cause I thought I baked you a cake.

VALERIE: The heck?

GAIL: For my poor brother Frank. The Gail of last week would've stuck this in your neck, but I'm a better person now. I even asked at the hospital, if I were to hypothetically stab somebody, where would be a good place so I wouldn't kill them. Say what you will about healthcare in this country, I have found doctors nothing but courteous and helpful. So that's that. We're fair and square now, Valerie. I forgive you for whatever you did to Frank. I forgive you.

(GAIL *holds her hand out to* VALERIE. VALERIE *takes her hand and they shake.*)

GAIL: Yeah…that's what I thought.

(GAIL *tosses* VALERIE'*s hand aside, disgusted.*)

You wouldn't've shook my hand for forgiveness if you didn't feel the need for my forgiveness, so you know what I'm forgiving you for? I'm forgiving you for *nothing.* I *don't* forgive you. You did something and you feel guilty and I will never forgive you.

(GAIL *exits the kitchen, slamming the door.* MIDGE *gets the gallon of blood from the fridge.*)

MIDGE: Heard a rumor round town you butchered him. Chopped off his hands, mailed 'em to Hong Kong. Chopped off his feet, fed 'em to polar bears at the zoo.

Stabbed him in the neck with a meat thermometer.
Wrenched open an artery, drained the hot blood out of
him. Didn't spill a drop.

(MIDGE sets down the gallon of blood.)

VALERIE: The gossip in this town. Shouldn't believe
everything you hear, you know that. *(Pause)* You never
told me what happened out on that lake with your
dad. You came home and he wasn't with you. You
never told me what happened.

MIDGE: You know why I never told you?

VALERIE: Why?

MIDGE: You never asked.

(Pause)

VALERIE: What happened?

MIDGE: He just left.

VALERIE: That's it?

MIDGE: Walked off into the night.

VALERIE: He should've called. Why wouldn't he at least
call to tell us he's all right?

MIDGE: I don't know, Mom.

VALERIE: God. Lots of ways to kill a person, no death
worse than a heartbreak to drive them away into that
cold lonely night. I am guilty. And I'm going to get
away with it.

END OF PLAY

CPSIA information can be obtained at www.ICGtesting.com
Printed in the USA
LVOW10s1314161016

508986LV00015B/181/P